First published in the United Kingdom in 2005
By HandE Publishers Ltd
Epping Film Studios, Brickfield Business Centre, Thornwood High Road,
Epping, Essex CM16 6TH

Illustrated by Neil Slater

Type set by Lynn Jones

A CIP catalogue record for this book is available from
The British Library

IBSN 0-9548518-1-1

First printed and bound in 2006 by
Kowa Stationery Ltd,16-18 Hing
Yip St,Kwun Tong,Kowloon,HK

My first car

Logo designed by Chris Crew
As seen through his eyes

It took Chris five years to put this book together and he would like to thank
all who contributed their stories to it.

HandE Publishers

Dedication

To My Mother, Ethel Crew

Contents

Chris Crew

The simple things in life are free, though for the author of this book Christopher Crew some have come at a high price.

Born on 22 December 1949 in Nottingham Chris' first steps in life were an exciting adventure just like any other child. Yet taking the leap from his mothers arms into the big wide world of school changed all that. In his own words, 'These were the worst years of my life,' he said, 'I was bullied and picked on because I couldn't read or write. It was for that reason I played truant most of the time. School governors and teachers put all this down to behaviour problems and not my learning abilities; although we must remember that dyslexia wasn't recognised as a disorder in those days and as a boy telling teachers 'I cant do it' wasn't acceptable.'

It was in the late 60's when Chris was moved to Rose Hill Special School in Nottingham to help with his academic needs. Unfortunately they also didn't recognise his disorder. 'No one seemed to understand why I couldn't read or write and I couldn't explain what I was experiencing being faced with this word blindness.'

After leaving school Chris followed the path far away from his academic disability and joined the entertainment industry. As a compere and all round entertainer in the famous Red Coat of Butlins he entertained holiday makers all over the country.

It wasn't until eight years ago in 1998 he attended the University of Bangor where he underwent numerous tests. They found conclusively that Chris had a total of seventeen counts of dyslexia. 'Maybe if they had known this when I was younger my life may have taken a different path.'

His inspiration for this book isn't a happy, spur of the moment idea. In fact it could be said that it has been a life changing moment. 'Dyslexia has been the bane of my life and seven years ago I reached the end of the road. I was on the brink of suicide, not knowing which way to turn I wanted to end my life.'

'It was midnight when I made my way to Bull Bay Cliffs where I planned to do just that,' he said, 'I know that most suicide is seen as a cowards way out but in fact being a coward was one reason I didn't jump.'

'So many thoughts ran through my head, the hurt I would bring to my wife and children and the confusion I would have left behind.

It wasn't until I got close to the edge I realised I wasn't as desperate as I thought - I realised throwing myself down would probably hurt!'

'I strolled home, sat back in my favourite chair and instead threw my thoughts back to the beginning of my life. Reflecting and trying to figure out what made me get to this breaking point. I never did figure this out as my first car, a Bull nose Morris Oxford, 501 NIK, stuck in my memory.'

'Few things in life trip us into the nostalgia mode more that first hunk of metal we acquired and which, years later, can still inflame the emotions and send us racing back to a milestone in our lives'.

'Love them or hate them, our first cars are seldom forgotten and we all have a different story to tell. Some remember them as their pride and joy, gave them pet names and enjoyed fleeting love affairs, though separation and the scrap yard were often just around the corner'.

'Others still recoil at the embarrassment of their rust bucket on wheels and being one step ahead of the law. Nevertheless more than that, our first car, that we chose, what we could afford, what we acquired from necessity, what we were given by well meaning relatives reveal much of where we came from and what we once were'.

Celebrities, stars, actors, public figures and MP's have all contributed to this fantastic book which, for most gives a tantalising glimpse of their early beginnings before they were famous.

My inspiration

Brian Conley

First car: Citroen estate

You would expect an entertainer with the comic touch to have humourous recollections of his first car and Brian Conley does not disappoint.

Having purchased the brown car from his uncle at the age of 21 in 1982, it was soon branded the 'Turd Mobile'.

The strange-coloured Citroen was not exactly in the passion wagon category and Brian traded it in for a sleeker vehicle, one of the earliest Ford Escort XR3s, after a year when his career took off.

'It was a horrible looking colour and all my friends called it the 'Turd Mobile', funnily enough it wasn't a hit with the ladies,' He says.

Yet he does have some happy memories of the cumbersome brown wagon. The model had a special suspension raising gear which once allowed him to make his escape from a locked car park in Poole where he had been in Panto with Anita Harris.

'I was faffing about in the dressing room and when I came out the car park was locked with my car in it,' says Brian. 'There was a small wall all the way round it about 2ft high. I kicked a bit down so I could get my car wheel up to it.

'I put the car into this gear so it lifted up and I was able to drive out. If it wasn't for that car I would have been stuck in Poole for Xmas. 'I could not forget my first car, it helped me out in my early days and I will certainly never ever forget that colour!'

Brian is dyslexic but is living proof of how it has not prevented him from reaching the top of his chosen profession.

'I went for a test when I was 23 and suddenly realised I was not thick,' he says. 'The wife Anne-Marie does the writing and I take care of other stuff. I am lucky I have a talent and it is almost as if dyslexia makes you good at other things so I am happy.'

Profile:
One of the nation's most loved entertainers on stage and screen, Brian has been an actor and presenter since he was 12. He has appeared in eight Royal Variety Performances and received a Silver Heart Award from the Variety Club of Great Britain.

He has starred in West End shows, Me and My Girl at the Adelphi Theatre, Jolson at the Victoria Palace Theatre and most recently Caractacas Potts in the smash hit musical Chitty Chitty Bang Bang at the London Palladium. His TV credits include This Way Up (LWT), The Brian Conley Show (LWT), Time After Time ITV and pr esenting the National Lottery Show BBC. He is also r enowned for his pantomime performances.

My first car

'It was a horrible looking colour and all my friends called it the 'Turd Mobile', funnily enough it wasn't a hit with the ladies.'

Julian Lloyd Webber

First car: 850cc Mini

Perhaps a Mini is not the perfect car to be transporting a cello.

That was certainly the case for internationally-renowned cellist Julian Lloyd Webber who also happened to bizarrely be storing two dead pheasants on his back seat after driving home from one of his earliest concerts.

The organisers of the concert in Cambridge decided to give him two large but decidedly dead pheasants as thanks for his efforts and he put them alongside his cello in the car.

Unfortunately Julian was stopped by the police on the way home because one of the rear lights on his Mini was not working. He found it hard to convince the boys in blue of the authenticity of his back seat load.

The officer peered at the shadowy forms on the rear seat and asked the young cellist what he was carrying.

'Why, two pheasants and a cello,' he replied innocently.

The officer then boomed: 'May I remind you that it is an offence to obstruct a police officer in the course of his duty. I will ask you again what are you carrying in the back?'

Julian explains the finale to the bizarre encounter. 'I got out and let the crestfallen officer discover the ugly truth for himself!'

Profile:
Widely regarded as one of the most creative musicians of his generation, Julian Lloyd Webber has collaborated with an extraordinary array of musicians from Yehudi Menuhin, Lorin Maazel, Neville Marriner and Georg Solti to Stephane Grappelli, Elton John and Cleo Laine.

Julian has made many outstanding recordings including his Brit- Award winning Elgar Concerto conducted by Yehudi Menuhin, the Dvorák Concerto with Vaclav Neumann and the Czech Philharmonic, Tchaikovsky's Rococo Variations with the London Symphony under Maxim Shostakovich and a coupling of Britten's Cello Symphony and Walton's Concerto with Sir Neville Marriner and the Academy of St Martin in the Fields. Julian has also recorded several highly successful CD's of short pieces for Universal Classics including Made In England, Cello Moods, and Cradle Song.

My first car

'I got out and let the crestfallen officer discover the ugly truth for himself!'

Kaye Wragg

First car: Ford Fiesta

Actress Kaye Wragg caused quite a stir when she was out driving in her first car but it was not the vehicle that got the admiring glances.

Because as she willingly admits her blue Ford Fiesta - bought second-hand from a friend's parents' for £400 - was a bit of a rust bucket.

'It was at least 10 years old but I had it for two years, it never broke down and it was called Pee Poo,' she says.

'It was knackered and very rusty but I loved it and couldn't watch the day the men came to take it away to be crushed.'

Kaye had a mini-disk stereo installed which cost more than the car itself.

One summer she was driving around in Camden, North London when a by-passer spotted her in the Fiesta with the music blaring out.

'He looked at me, at the car, back at me, and said, 'Man, that car's a wreck, the music and the girl are great, but the wreck's putting you down', explains Kaye.

'I was gutted, I was really insulted that my car had taken a verbal beating but the man was quite cute, otherwise he would have got a mouthful off me!'

Profile:
Cheshire-born Kaye is most well known for playing nurse Kate Oakley in Channel 4 comedy drama No Angels and recently starred in the BBC drama A Thing Called Love. Her many other television credits include Where the Heart Is, Dalziel and Pascoe, The Bill, Mersey Beat, Holby City, Wire in the Blood, The Lakes. She also appeared in the television adaptation of Jake Arnott's The Long Firm.

Now drives:
A Toyota Yaris 'with personalised dents, scratches and you name it to make it more mine.

'No man will ever call it names and if they did I think I'd have to run over their toe to teach them a lesson.'

My first car

'It was knackered and very rusty but I loved it and couldn't watch the day the men came to take it away to be crushed.'

Harry Carpenter

As the nation's best-loved boxing commentator Harry Carpenter is always in top gear.

But his first car, a yellow Hillman Minx bought in 1954, had its gear lever on the steering column and it is not a feature he remembers with much joy.

One night, on his way home from a boxing event, the gear linkage broke way out in the Surrey countryside near Dorking.

Harry, who was 29 at the time and a boxing writer for the Daily Mail, explains: 'I had all sorts of problems finding a garage that would mend it at that time of night and I seem to remember not getting home until the small hours.'

He had bought the Hillman after his father had introduced him to a car dealer named Norman Kane, from whom he continued to buy cars from for many years after.

'The business part was always conducted in the White Horse pub, just across the road from showrooms in Peckham Rye, South London,' explains Harry.

Shortly after the Hillman gear breakdown, he swapped it for a vintage Riley 2.6 which uniquely had its gear lever mounted on the right hand side of the driver's seat.

Profile:
Harry Carpenter has been the undisputed voice of boxing for the best part of 50 years.

After two years in the navy, Harry originally joined the BBC in 1949 and delivered his first boxing commentary in the same year. He mixed working for the BBC, the Greyhound Express and the Daily Mail before switching to television full time in 1962.

Harry presented the midweek sports magazine Sports-night and also worked on BBC radio throughout his career. For much of the 1970s and '80s he co-hosted the Sports Personality of the Year, having first contributed to the programme in 1958.

He, perhaps, became best known for his magnetic double act with Frank Bruno, but he also enjoyed a notable relationship with the boxing great Mohammad Ali.

Now drives:
A Mercedes E300 Diesel Estate 'A 3-litre job. This carries my wife and I, a lot of luggage, very quietly and efficiently along the French motorways to our hideaway house in south-western France.'

My first car

'I had all sorts of problems finding a garage that would mend it at that time of night and I seem to remember not getting home until the small hours.'

Sir Chris Bonington

First car: Mini van

For someone with such a great head for the world's heights you would have thought mountaineering legend Chris Bonington would have started his driving life in something more grandiose than a Mini.

Admittedly it was a van but the small vehicle was constantly overloaded with climbing gear as Chris drove around on expeditions, including two to the Alps.

He and his wife Wendy bought it in 1963 with the proceeds he earnt from writing about his team's first British ascent of the North Wall of the Eiger.

'It was our sole possession. We were living in furnished rented accommodation in the Lakes and had very little cash at the time,' he says.

'The registration was AMM - I forget the numbers - A and we called her Amelia.' And there is no doubt that Amelia served the mountaineering great with all the grit and determination he himself showed in climbing the world's highest peaks.

'I drove her for 150,000 miles between 1963 and 1966. My mileage was colossal driving to lectures,' Chris explains. 'It stood us in wonderful stead and I was very fond of her.'

My first car

Profile:
Sir Chris Bonington is one of the world's best known mountaineers and explorers. In 1975 he led a successful British expedition to climb the south-west face of Everest. Thirteen years later at the age of 50 and on his fourth Everest expedition, he finally reached the summit of the world's highest mountain himself. As well as Mount Everest, Sir Chris has successfully conquered some of the most notorious and formidable mountains across the globe, and is still mountaineering into his 70s.

'It stood us in wonderful stead and I was very fond of her.'

Bruce Forsyth OBE

First car: Ford 8

Can you remember them? Cuddly toy, record player, washing machine, cutlery set...Ford 8.

Yes showbiz legend Bruce Forsyth's first car would truly be at home in his most famous show the Generation Game on that beloved conveyor belt.

He bought it 60 years ago and although he cannot remember how much it cost he does remember the number plate ELR 804.

He will also never forget temporarily losing touch with it after it was stolen from Leicester Square in London's West End in the days when you could still park there.

'It was later found in Plaistow, East London and they did leave the 4 wheels!' he says.'Nobody ended up buying it from me but they did buy the wheels.'

And suffice to say that Bruce's subsequent motors have had a tad more speed about them.

'I now drive a Bentley and a golf buggy. The buggy goes faster than my old Ford 8!'

Profile:
Bruce Forsyth is an entertainer and showman who achieved celebrity status on the show Saturday Night at the London Palladium, and has since presented game shows such as The Price is Right, Play Your Cards Right, The Generation Game and You Bet.

Known for his catch phrases, 'Nice to see you, to see you nice', 'Give us a twirl Anthea', 'It's gonna be a good night tonight if you play your cards right', 'Good game, good game' and 'Brucie Bonus'.

Bruce Forsyth is one of the U.K.'s most loved and durable stars and has been in show business for more than sixty years. It is a career that began very young when, in the middle of World War Two, he left school and aged 14 began performing professionally billed as Boy Bruce The Mighty Atom.

Sixteen years later in 1958, he became an 'overnight' star when he was chosen to host Sunday Night At The London Palladium and he has remained one of the most influential and popular performers on British television ever since. On New Years Day 2004, BBC2 devoted an evening to him, including showing an extended version of his hosting Have I Got News For You.

In 1998, he was awarded the O.B.E. for his services to the entertainment industry.

Now drives:
A Bentley and that buggy to make it easier for him to play his favourite hobby golf.

My first car

'I now drive a Bentley and a golf buggy. The buggy goes faster than my old Ford 8!'

Lord James Callaghan

First car: 1921 model Wolseley Drophead Coupe

Driving was a beautiful ordeal when former Prime Minister James Callaghan set out in his first car.

He and his wife Audrey purchased the 11.9 horsepower Wolseley Drophead Coupe in 1935 for the princely sum of £8 10s.

'We used it regularly for weekend jaunts including a summer holiday in Cornwall. It always took us there and back safely,' he says.

'The battery was on the running board and the car had gleaming brass fittings and headlights which we used to polish lovingly at the weekends.'

Although, as he explains, It was a bit of an ordeal just to get the car going.'

'In those days two of the principal tasks were how to use a starting handle without breaking your thumb, and secondly it was essential to learn how to double declutch, an art that I guess has been mostly forgotten now!'

Profile:

Former Prime Minister Jim Callaghan died in March 2005 aged 92.

Lord Callaghan entered 10 Downing Street as Prime Minister in 1976 following the resignation of Harold Wilson. He took office aged 64 and spent 3 years and 29 days as Prime Minister.

In a statement paying tribute to Lord Callaghan after his death, Prime Minister Tony Blair said, 'He came to deserve and receive great respect as a leader and as a man'.

The son of a naval chief petty officer, James Callaghan left school at 14. He worked as a tax officer and was later employed by the TUC.

After serving in World War Two he was elected as a Labour MP for Cardiff South in the post-war Labour landslide, and later represented Cardiff South East.

'The battery was on the running board and the car had gleaming brass fittings and headlights which we used to polish lovingly at the weekends.'

Burt Kwouk

First car: Ford Phaeton

As someone forever famous for playing the comically destructive Cato in the Peter Sellers Pink Panther films, you would expect actor Burt Kwouk's first car to be a little different.

It was a 1936 blue Ford Phaeton, a four-door convertible which he bought in New York in 1949.

'I used it for four years at university in the US and I sold it in 1955,' he says. 'It was just an old banger which served me well.'

Profile:
Burt Kwouk was born in Manchester in July 1930.

He has appeared in an enormous number of films and TV programmes over the years and is perhaps most famous for playing Cato, Inspector-Clouseau's man-servant in the Pink Panther films. Alongside comic great Peter Sellers the pair enjoyed a series of hilarious scenes in which Cato attempted to beat Clouseau in combat.

He has appeared in many other British TV programmes including recently Channel 4s Banzai and BBC1s Last of the Summer Wine and Doctor Who.

My first car

'It was just an old banger which served me well.'

Sally Lindsay

First car: Hyundai Pony

Many of us give our car a name and Coronation Street actress Sally Lindsay is no different.

She tagged her first car Colin Bell after the Manchester City striker. The C reg Hyundai Pony was even pale 'City' blue and 'went like a rocket', just like the star footballer.

'I was 24 years old and I loved it,' says Sally. 'My best friend Charlotte gave it to me and I toured the country in it in a theatre show.

'However, the radiator was clapped out so I had to break an egg in it, as I couldn't afford Radweld to block the leak. The top had also gone missing so, I had to use a half potato for that too!'

Profile:
Known and loved by the British public as Shelley Unwin - the owner/barmaid of the famous Rover's Return in Coronation Street, Sally can also be seen at the beginning of her close friend Peter Kay's live video.

Now drives:
A Mini Cooper still called Colin.

My first car

'However, the radiator was clapped out so I had to break an egg in it, as I couldn't afford Radweld to block the leak. The top had also gone missing, so I had to use a half potato for that too!'

Colin Baker

First car: Austin 16

As Doctor Who Colin Baker was famed for getting himself out of trouble but his first car proved un-saveable.

He had it just a week and was driving out of London towards Manchester where he lived when it blew up.

'There was a loud bang from under the bonnet, it juddered to a stop, the roof rack slid forward and all my suitcases, which were on it slid off on to the A1 in Hendon,' he says.

'A local garage told me how much it would cost to repair the engine. I went home on the train and never saw my prized possession again.'

The car's untimely death may not have been too much of a surprise though.

'It was a second (or probably 37th) hand Austin 16,' he explains. 'I bought it for hardly anything - in fact they may have paid me to take it!'

...HO HO HO HA HA HA HE HE HE....

Profile:
Colin Baker is an English actor and voice over artist who is best known for playing the sixth incarnation of the Doctor in the long-running science fiction television series Doctor Who, from 1984 to 1986.

After leaving Doctor Who he continued to act, mainly on the stage although he has had many star appearances in many TV dramas.

My first car

'A local garage told me how much it would cost to repair the engine. I went home on the train and never saw my prized possession again.'

Alexei Sayle

First car: Fiat 124

Comedian Alexei Sayle's first car experience could easily become subject matter for a stand-up routine.

Aged 28, he paid an Oxfordshire farmer £100 for the dark blue Fiat with a look that he describes as 'classic three box' as it really did look like three boxes stuck together.

Driving it did not prove to be as easy as the purchase however. 'The sensible thing to do next would have been to have some driving lessons, but that would have been too easy in those crazee 1970s times when our minds were as flared as our trousers,' he says. 'Instead my idea was to buy a cheap car that I would drive around while friends who already possessed driving licences sat with me as I learnt.'

He arranged for a friend to drive the car back to Fulham where he lived at the time. Unfortunately the friend had a dog who liked eating car seats!

'The place we lived in was on the 12th floor of a council tower block but even that height looking down we could clearly see the huge gouts of yellow foam that had been torn form the rear bench,' he explains.

Alexei was still excited by his purchase and decided to move it to a better parking space. 'Starting it up and pulling out slightly, a car came up behind me and hooted,' he says. 'In a panic I drove into the road and, with the other car pursuing me, headed off up the street.'

'Although I just about knew how to drive straight ahead in second gear, I didn't know how to change up or down, stop without stalling, or turn around. 'In a terrified sweat, I hatched a plan, figuring that if I could just get to Hammersmith roundabout, mile and a half away, without stopping and go all the way round it, I would then be heading back to my house.'

'I was away for over two hours. My wife was going frantic because of reports coming in over the radio of huge traffic jams all over west London that were being caused by a particularly slow-moving vehicle.'

My first car

Funnily enough Alexei's acquaintance with the Fiat 124 did not last much longer. 'There appeared to be a distinct shortage of friends who wanted to go for pointless seven mile an hour drives with me in my car with torn seats covered in dog slobber,' he says. 'In the end, I gave it to a musician friend of mine who didn't want it and left it in a car park. And then I did the sensible thing and booked myself in for some proper driving lessons.'

Profile:

Alexei is best known as a comedian and his part in cult series The Young Ones. He also starred in The Comic Strip Presents, The All New Alexei Sayle Show and Alexei Sayle's Merry-go-round.

He has written several scripts for TV shows, has a regular column in The Independent newspaper and a novel 'Overtaken' under his belt.

Photo: Andy Hollingworf

'There appeared to be a distinct shortage of friends who wanted to go for pointless seven mile an hour drives with me in my car, with torn seats covered in dog slobber.'

Martyn Davies

First car: Austin Mini

Maybe a little red Austin is not the best first car to drive when you are 6ft 3in tall!

ITV weather forecaster Martyn Davies adopted a special sitting technique, to ensure he could fit into the small vehicle.

'My friends were amazed I could fit into it because I'm very tall,' he says, 'but there was plenty of room for me. Though the driver's seat was so far back I was almost looking out of the rear passenger window!'

Martyn has fond memories of the vehicle in which he started his driving life.

'I remember my first car very well. I can even remember the registration number, it was JOE218E,' he explains.

'It was one of the old style Minis with the very long and wobbly gear stick, but I loved it.'

Profile:
A fully qualified meteorologist, Martyn Davies has been presenting ITV weather for more than 15 years, both regionally and nationally.

My first car

Martyn Davies

'It was one of the old style Minis with the very long and wobbly gear stick but I loved it.'

Julie Hesmondhalgh

First car: Fiat Uno

The security guards at the gate on the Coronation Street studios used to laugh at actress Julie Hesmondhalgh for her choice of first car.

The little blue F reg Fiat Uno was perhaps a little understated for a star on one of Britain's most popular TV programmes.

She bought the car - named Betty - from her cousin Steve's second hand car salesroom when she first joined 'Corrie' in 1998 and had a big row with her dad who did not think she could afford it.

'The security guards used to laugh at me and reckoned she Betty would last me two months before I'd come rolling in in a brand new Merc,' she says.

'30,000 miles and two-and-a-half years later and I finally parted with her, giving her to my friend and neighbour so I still see her every day!'

Profile:
After success as an amateur stage actress, Julie was asked to play Hayley in ITV1s Coronation Street.

Hayley was originally only intended to be short-term character, as a love interest for Roy. But tremendous positive public reaction to Hayley, and her on-screen chemistry with Roy, convinced the producers to make her a regular cast member.

She has rapidly become one of Britain's favourite TV actresses.

Now drives:
A red Mini Cooper and a bright pink Camper van called Lola.

My first car

Keep on truckin'!
Lots of love,
Julie Hesmondhalgh x

'30,000 miles and two-and-a-half years later and I finally parted with her, giving her to my friend and neighbour so I still see her every day!'

Eric Knowles

First car: Renault 4

Having a sunroof on your car is a nice luxury except for when it almost blows off and your other half has to hang onto it as you go down the motorway!

Professional antiquarian Eric Knowles's first car was a bright yellow Renault 4 1971 complete with a full length black fabric sunroof, which he had bought from the neighbour of a work colleague for £350.

The car - chistened Yellow Peril - had one of those 'push me pull you' umbrella handle gear levers and 'sunroof'.

'The entire sunroof blew off the first time I took it on the motorway and across to the Isle of Wight,' explains Eric.

'My wife Anita had to hang on to the sunroof for the remainder of our three day holiday.' The following Christmas a spot of black ice and a slide into a lamppost caused another near terminal problem for the Yellow Peril.

'My dad's amazing car mechanic brought it back from the dead about 3 months later,' explains Eric. 'I eventually traded it in for a 1979 Renault 14 (red with go faster black stripe) before the year was out - the year being 1981.'

Profile:
As well as being a recognised expert in his chosen field, Eric Knowles is now a well-known face in the world of antiques, particularly to viewers of the BBC's Antiques Road Show.

He has also appeared in Crimewatch UK, Selling the Family Silver, Going for a Song, The Great Antiques Hunt, The Antiques Inspectors,'It's a Gift, You Can't Take It With You, Jim Davidson's Generation Game and Countdown.

'The entire sunroof blew off the first time I took it on the motorway and across to the Isle of Wight.'

Joe Pasquale

First car: Ford Anglia 1961

For a picture of comedian Joe Pasquale in his first car think Brylcreem and Heartbeat.

He had just passed his driving test when he bought the Ford Anglia for £75. It was just like the well known car in the popular ITV1 series Heartbeat except its colour was blue.

'It was a great little car and I had so much fun owning it, it is definitely right to say that everyone remembers their first car!' Joe says.

'It brings back so many memories like palm toffee, getting ready on a Saturday night to go out and putting plenty of Brylcreem on my hair.'

My first car

Profile:
Squeaky-voiced Joe remains one of Britain's top 'live' touring comedians and regularly sells out shows around the country.

He is also rumoured to be a favourite of the Royal family, which goes some way in explaining his many Royal Variety performances.

Despite writing 'The Big Thick Joe Pasquale Book' and appearing in his own TV show during the 90s, Joe's big time break came when he won the ITV reality series 'I'm A Celebrity Get Me Out Of Here'.

His latest TV appearance has been presenting the new series of 'The Price is Right'.

Joe Pasquale

'It brings back so many memories like palm toffee, getting ready on a Saturday night to go out and putting plenty of Brylcreem on my hair.'

Jeremy Vine

First car: Ford Escort

Some people worship their first car, others just have to put up with a passed-on battered wreck.

That was the fate of TV and radio presenter Jeremy Vine when he bought his primary motor as a Durham University student.

'The previous owner had given it 'a roar' which sounded good but it meant the engine was defeaning and it gulped petrol,' says Jeremy. 'Because the Ford was brown my university friends nicknamed it the 'moving turd'. In the end I was glad to have it stolen!'

Jeremy Vine has presented the Politics Show since its launch at the start of 2003.

At the same time he also took over the news and music slot Jimmy Young had occupied on BBC Radio 2 for 29 years, opening the new programme by playing Thunder Road by Bruce Springsteen.

My first car

'Because the Ford was brown my university friends nicknamed it the 'moving turd'. In the end I was glad to have it stolen!'

George Carey

First car: Morris A30

Every parent knows the perils of a long car journey with young children on board.

Former Archbishop of Canterbury and now Lord Carey of Clifton, George and his wife Eileen had one such nightmare trip in their Morris A30 which already had 110,000 miles on the clock when they bought it in 1963.

They had three children at the time under the age of three and were taking them up to Scotland to visit relatives.

'On our very first outing following the purchase of the car we had a lovely run up to Scotland and it was just as we were crossing the border in the middle of nowhere that the car broke down,' explains Dr Carey.

'We slept uncomfortably in the car with three children for several hours until the AA were able to find us and get us started again.'

'It is not an experience I would want to repeat.'

Profile:
From humble working class origins George Carey rose to become the most senior bishop in the Church of England.

When he became the 103rd Archbishop of Canterbury in 1991, he was the first not to have attended Oxford or Cambridge universities.

My first car

Photo: Eleanor Bentall

To Chris
with warm regards
George Carey
Archbishop of Canterbury . 1991 – 2002

'On our very first outing following the purchase of the car we had a lovely run up to Scotland and it was just as we were crossing the border in the middle of nowhere that the car broke down.'

June Whitfield

First car: Austin Seven

Parking your car nowadays is never easy on Britain's cluttered streets.

But for actress June Whitfield it was a piece of cake. She was able to park her Austin Seven right outside the stage door in London's West End.

'I travelled to London each night when I was in South Pacific in 1951 and parked near the stage door!' she explains. 'I don't think you could do that now!'

Profile:

June Whitfield is the Grandmother of British comedy. Well, she has played one of comedy's most famous grandmothers in Absolutely Fabulous.

She began her career as an actress in London's West End, then moved to radio in 1953, appearing on Take It From Here.

June's career has seen success in theatre, pantomime, film and television. A regular cast member of the Carry On... series through the 1970s, it was in 1979 that June Whitfield found huge popularity alongside Terry Scott in the long-running sit-com Terry and June.

TV fame struck twice when she was cast as June Monsoon in Absolutely Fabulous in 1992. Playing the scene-stealing ditzy grandmother.

My first car

'I travelled to London each night when I was in South Pacific in 1951 and parked near the stage door!'

The Two Ronnies

First car: A Bullnosed Morris Ronnie Corbett and a Bike Ronnie Barker

Ronnie Corbett is a man who enjoys attention to detail so it is no surprise he remembers his first car well.

'My first car was a bullnosed Morris, navy blue, black wings and brown leather upholstery for which I paid £75,' he says. 'I bought it from the stagedoor keeper of the Palace Theatre, Manchester when I was doing a season there.'

'I suppose I got it in about 1957 or 58 and kept it for about a year while I was doing Crackerjack.'

'I remember I used to drive to rehearsals in it, so it wasn't too much of an embarrassment but I enjoyed it greatly.'

And as for partner in comedy Ronnie Barker, well you would not expect anything different than an unusual answer to the question: 'What do you remember about your first car?'

The comic genius replied: 'I cannot tell you about my first car because my first car was a bike.' And who can argue with that!

My first car

Profile:
For the tenure of their long BBC run, The Two Ronnies - Messrs Barker and Corbett - were second only to Morecambe and Wise as the best-rated comedy double-act on British TV.

Not that they were in any sense competing or overshadowed - The Two Ronnies has long established its claim as one of the most successful British comedy shows of them all; safe, yes, but often very funny and of vast majority appeal. 'With a good night from him and a good night from me'.

Corbett was also successful in 'Sorry'; and Barker in Open All Hours and Porridge.

'My first car was a bullnosed Morris, navy blue, black wings and brown leather upholstery for which I paid £75.'

Paul Burrell

First car: Renault

He may have been Princess Diana's 'rock' but his first car experience was a little less resolute.

Former butler Paul Burrell's first motor - a white Renault - was given to him by his dad as he and wife Maria could not afford their own.

And it is Maria who outlines its unreliability. 'It was always breaking down,' she recalls.

'The most memorable time was when we went to have a look at our new house down at Highgrove, Gloucs Prince Charles' home, before starting work for the Prince and Princess of Wales.

'After spending most of the day there we headed up the M5 north to Cheshire to spend some time with my mum.'

'We were about 30 miles from home when all of a sudden the car swirved all over the place.'

'The wheel had come off the car, luckily Paul managed to steer the car onto the hard shoulder and we spent the rest of the journey in a breakdown lorry.'

'Our son Alexander thought it was great fun as he was only 2

years old at the time. I'm afraid to say that was the end of the white Renault. Paul decided it was time for a new car!'

Profile:
Paul Burrell spent 21 years as a devoted servant to the Queen, Prince Charles and finally Diana.

He claims to have been the late Princess' most loyal servant, becoming a shoulder for her to cry on as her marriage to Prince Charles disintegrated.

In 2002 he was cleared of theft charges after the Queen dramatically intervened his Old Bailey trial to confirm that she had given him permission to keep some of Diana's possessions.

My first car

'The wheel had come off the car, luckily Paul managed to steer the car onto the hard shoulder and we spent the rest of the journey in a breakdown lorry'.

Anne Robinson

First car: Soft Top MG

She may be the Queen of Mean but a spot of motherly love set Anne Robinson on her road to fame.

The Weakest Link host bought her first car, a British Racing Green MG, with £800 sent to her by her mother.

The letter read 'Pet, here is £800 to buy a car, love mummy'. Anne drove to her first interview as a journalist in the car. She took her dog with her for luck.

It worked, she got the job and as they say the rest is history.

Profile:
Anne Robinson became the highest paid woman journalist in Britain in a glittering career which started off at the Daily Mail and went on to The Mirror, The Sun, Today and The Times.

She rose to TV fame on consumer programme Watchdog and Points of View but really hit the big time presenting the quiz show The Weakest Link in which she reduces contestants to tatters with the send-off line 'You are the weakest link goodbye!'

'You are the weakest link goodbye!'

Dame Judi Dench

First car: 1938 MG

There's nothing like a dame and Judi Dench would certainly have caught the eye in her first car.

She bought the sporty MG from Douglas Harris when they were both at the Old Vic in 1958 and even admits to driving it for some time without a licence!

'It was a convertible sports car and I never learned how to put the roof on,' she said. 'So I had to wear a mackintosh and hat whenever it rained.'

Profile:
As if singlehandedly setting out to prove that actresses aren't necessarily finished when they reach A Certain Age, Dame Judi Dench achieved her greatest fame and loudest plaudits while in her mid-sixties.

Formerly known as one of the UK's finest Shakespearians, once she'd taken to screen acting in earnest she was continually Oscar-nominated, for her roles in Mrs Brown, Shakespeare In Love, Chocolat and Iris, and all of this despite a general aversion to film-making.

'It was a convertible sports car and I never learned how to put the roof on.'

Tim Healy

The phrase 'passion wagon' will be familiar with many motorists and their passengers!

Like many people's first cars, actor Tim Healy was proud as punch with his especially because of its pulling potential.

Bought in 1972 for the princely sum of £85, the Riley Elf proved to be a winner in the dating game for young Tim.

'It made it a lot easier to get a girl when you had a car and could take her home after a night out. I must admit it was a bit of a passion wagon,' he says.

Profile:
Tim Healy found fame as Dennis the gaffer of Auf Wiedershen Pet 'magnificent seven' back in the 1980s.

Since then, the Geordie actor has starred in many TV dramas, including The Grand and Common as Muck. He was recently reunited with his former colleagues for two new series of Auf Wiedershen Pet.

'It made it a lot easier to get a girl when you had a car and could take her home after a night out. I must admit it was a bit of a passion wagon.'

Henry Sandon

Everyone has a name for their car even if they do not admit it in public.

Antiques Roadshow ceramics expert Henry Sandon is no different. He and his wife called his first car - a second hand Morris 8 - Lana after the film actress Lana Morris.

But there was another reason for the name.

'You had to use a starting handle to turn the engine on and there was another famous film star called Lana Turner. So the car had 2 names!' he explains.

'It had a dreadful habit of conking out on a steep hill and I had to thump the petrol pump with a spanner to get it going again.'

'But it was a fun car and I was very proud of it. I have had lots of cars since but they have not had the character of Lana.'

My first car

'You had to use a starting handle to turn the engine on and there was another famous film star called Lana Turner. So the car had 2 names!'

Charles Ingram

First car: Morris Minor 1100cc

Who wants to be a millionaire when you have got a beloved Morris Minor to drive? Charles Ingram the young student was certainly happy with his first wheels.

Charles, who was deprived of his £1 million win on the ITV gameshow commonly known as Millionaire after he was accused of listening to a friend's coughs in the crowd to answer questions, bought his first car in 1981 for £90 from 'someone in a caravan park in the Welsh valleys.'

Charles was studying A levels at Barry College and living with his father who was serving at RAF St Athan.

'It was a green, 4 door, Morris Minor 1100cc and it was superbly reliable, efficient and useful,' he says. 'But I was soon to discover that the floor was rotten and water would flood in when it was raining!

'With no money, I convinced a friend who was learning to be a welder to rebuild the floor for me. He welded on a new floor from above, and one from below, so it ended up being pretty solid with three floors.

'I spent a fortune on a black under seal and waxoil, a protective oily gunge that sealed the new underside from the elements.'

Despite the problems Charles loved the Morris.

'With wings falling off, and a multicolored paintwork consisting of the original green and lots of red oxide primer, and also a concourse boot lid which was the only part of the car I got around to properly restoring - that was painted British

racing green. My Moggy was highly recognisable throughout South Wales,' he recounts.

'I sold her in 1984 for £150 after about 30,000 miles. It was a wonderful car for a student as it was Group 1 insurance. It took my entire luggage and I could ferry people around.'

'Scrap yards were full of Moggies too, so spares were never a problem.'

Profile:
Major Charles Ingram was found guilty in 2003 of cheating his way to the top prize on Who Wants To Be a Millionaire.

During his trial for conspiracy to cheat the programme out of its £1m jackpot prize, a jury at Southwark Crown Court watched an unedited video recording of him making his way to the top that was never shown on TV.

Ingram was found guilty along with his wife Diana and college lecturer Tecwen Whittock of tricking game show host Chris Tarrant into signing the £1m cheque.

Since then he has tried his hand at a number of reality TV shows.

My first car

'It was a green, 4 door, Morris Minor 1100cc and it was superbly reliable, efficient and useful.'

Frank Carson

First car: Morris Oxford

You would expect Frank Carson's first car experience to be a bit madcap and it was.

'I had it three weeks and it suddenly started to rattle like the clappers,' says Frank.

'The guy I bought it off told me it was the ashtray moving about I could hear. Though two days later it conked out and that was the 'big end.' 'It cost me £650 and that was in 1952 - nowadays that would buy a scooter!'

BILL £650 (IT'S THE WAY WE TELL 'EM)

Profile:
Having been three times outright winner of the grandaddy of new talent talent shows, Opportunity Knocks, Frank rose to fame via the BBC's classic variety show, The Good Old Days and Granada TV's seminal series The Comedians. A record-breaking tour followed and the rest, as they say, is history.

Since those halcyon days, Frank has become one of the most televised comedians in Britain, with appearances on a long list of top-rated shows, not least of which was the 1992 Royal Variety Performance.

My first car

'I had it three weeks and it suddenly started to rattle like the clappers.'

Derek Fowlds

First car: Morris Minor Traveller

The popular Sunday evening TV show Heartbeat has reaquainted many of us with the gentle pace of life in the 60s.

Well for actor Derek Fowlds - who plays Oscar Blaketon in the long-running series - it also provides memories of his own first car.

For in the programme he drives around a blue Morris Minor Traveller, exactly the same model as his own first motor.

'It cost £350 and I loved driving it,' he says. 'They were happy days.'

Profile:

Derek Fowlds has played the role of Oscar Blaketon, one of the characters from the original novels on which Heartbeat is based, since the first series in 1991.

He started off as Aidensfield's police sergeant but was forced to retire due to health problems concerning his heart. He maintained his position in the community by running the village Post Office and now is even more prominent as the owner of the Aidensfield Arms.

My first car

'They were happy days.'

Bernard Cribbins

First car: Morris 1000

Mother-in-laws get a bad press but Bernard Cribbins does not believe the hype.

'Our first car was a Morris 1000 and we only got it because my mother-in-law gave us the money!' he admits. 'How about that for a different angle on mothers-in-law?'

Bernard did not even drive it either, preferring to be chauffeured around by his wife.

'I didn't drive in those days so my wife Gill acted as my driver,' he explains. 'We loved the car and whizzed all over the place in it.'

More recently Bernard has moved onto a Subaru Outback. 'I use it for fishing trips - if needs be I can sleep in the back!'

Profile:

Bernard Cribbins is one of the best known entertainers in the UK. He has been an actor since the age of 14, when he became a student player with his local repertory company.

By the 1950s, Cribbins had become a star of the London stage, featuring in his own revue. It wasn't until the 1960s, however, until he attained true public acclaim, appearing in a string of successful films including three Carry On's and had musical success with a number of novelty records like Right Said Fred and Hole in the Ground.

Cribbins' voice is known, of course, to millions around the world thanks to his narration of the immortal Wombles TV series. He was also the host of the popular game show Star Turn Challenge and appeared as aging lothario Wally Bannister in Coronation Street.

My first car

Best Wishes
Bernard Cribbins

'We loved the car and whizzed all over the place in it.'

Richard Pitman

First car: Morris Minor Estate

Many of us relied upon our parents to provide us with those first beloved wheels.

It was no different for horse racing legend Richard Pitman who was given his Morris Minor Estate by his father Jack shortly after his 17th birthday on Jan 21st 1960.

'It had been his pride and joy for many years but as I had just started working in racing stables near Cheltenham, he gave it to me to get the 7 miles to and from the stables,' says Richard. 'My mother Eve decided by midsummer of 1962 that I was safe enough to drive her from Cheltenham to London to visit relatives.'

'I was keen to show mother its paces so I opened the old girl up the car was called Molly and we were fairly flying along when my mother said 'It never sounded so good when your father drove it!'

'Within a minute one of the pistons went and some sort of rod came through the bonnet accompanied by crunching noises and much smoke! I had blown the engine up completely.'

'It took hours to be towed off the M4 and we got the coach back to Cheltenham and fray mother's nerves. I then had to bicycle the 14 miles daily to work before buying a new Mini on my 20th birthday.'

My first car

'I was keen to show mother its paces so I opened the old girl up (the car was called Molly) and we were fairly flying along when my mother said, 'It never sounded so good when your father drove it!'

Edwina Currie

First car: Austin 1100

That first car is nice to have but when you are young other neccesities come along - such as buying a house.

For Edwina Currie it meant selling her Austin 1100 which she bought in 1970 and describes as the 'standard little car of the time.'

'The Austin only lasted a year or so till I got engaged and then it was sold to raise the funds for a deposit,' she admits.

A new car was not long in arriving however as her career took off and she acquired a 'much posher' Wolseley 1300 with leather seats.

Profile:

Edwina Currie first stood for Parliament in 1983 and represented a Midlands seat for 14 years. She became one of the nation's best known MPs and served in Margaret Thatcher's government 1986-88, in the Department of Health. She resigned over food safety salmonella in December 1988.

She has published ten books. She started with non-fiction, then turned to novels which were instant best-sellers in the UK.

For five years she had her own very successful radio programme, 'Late Night Currie,' on BBC Radio 5 Live and has also been a TV presenter. She appeared in ITV's 'Hell's Kitchen' and was also winner of BBC TV's 'Celebrity Mastermind in 2004.' In ITV's 'The Big Call' July 2005 she helped one contestant win £20,000 and another almost £50,000 on Britain's National Lottery.

My first car

'The Austin only lasted a year or so till I got engaged and then it was sold to raise the funds for a deposit.'

Jono Coleman

First car: Fiat 124 Sport

It is a fact of life that your first car can often cost as much in repairs as it did to buy it.

For Jono Coleman the first year owning his 1969 red Fiat 124 sport cost him over 2,000 Australian dollars in repairs.

'It was a bit of a heap and came from a lady in Canberra, costing $2,000 Aus, but then I spent more than that in repairs,' he explains. 'It was a great red sports car but it would always overheat. I sold it for $1,500 Aus I think, or maybe less.'

An award-winning radio presenter, Australian Jono Coleman made his name on London radio station Heart 106.2 FM as a breakfast presenter. Since then he has worked for LBC and BBC London as well as reporting stints on GMTV and appearing on Celebrity Fit Club.

My first car

Photo: BBC

'It was a bit of a heap and came from a lady in Canberra, costing $2,000 Aus but then I spent more than that in repairs.'

Eric Morecambe

First car: Austin A70 Hereford

Legendary late comedian Eric Morecambe's first car experience is recounted by his devoted wife Joan.

'Both Eric and I started driving with Austin cars. Eric bought an Austin A70 Hereford in 1953 when I was expecting my first baby,' says Joan.'

'Until then I had not had driving lessons but I learnt while appearing in a summer season at Blackpool. We were actually living with his parents in Morecambe.'

'Then in 1957, or perhaps 1958, Eric bought me a little Austin A30. We toured all round the country in Eric's larger car during the days of Variety shows, travelling every Sunday.'

'My touring days ended once my second baby arrived, but Erics life in show business took a road off to huge success.'

Profile:
Eric Morecambe OBE, who died in 1984, was the stage name of Eric John Bartholomew.'

Eric Morecambe was a British comedian who together with Ernie Wise, formed the double act Morecambe and Wise. Eric took his stage name from the seaside resort of Morecambe in Lancashire, England - his home town. In the UK he is widely considered as a 'Comic Genius'.

Of all the comedy acts produced by the United Kingdom, Morecambe and Wise are arguably the best loved and most fondly remembered. They were perhaps the first truly great double act in the United Kingdom. Many have highlighted the genuine affection Eric and Ernie had for one other. Their enjoyment of their work was picked up by the audience who regarded them as friends as well as entertainers.

He and Wise were well-regarded and their reputation enabled them to garner a number of prestigious guests including Angela Rippon, Princess Anne, Cliff Richard, Glenda Jackson, Tom Jones, Elton John and even former Prime, Minister Harold Wilson. Des O'Connor was frequently the butt of their humour.

My first car

Photo: BBC

'My touring days ended once my second baby arrived.'

Tommy Walsh

First car: Morris 1000

Tommy Walsh's first car was offered to him at a knock-down price by a friend he describes as being 'involved in a somewhat dubious occupation.'

As a 17-year-old he spent £80 purchasing the Morris 1100 despite his mate having spent a fortune on it, including a new engine.

But he admits, 'it was one of those problem cars' and he eventually let it go for £30 to a 'little Maltese bloke' who was also into somewhat dubious dealings.

'I think I only owned the car for a couple of months before I was rid of it!' says Tommy. 'For me the vehicles I had to have in my work were commercials and my first real 'motor' was a twin-wheeled transit, for my landscape gardening business The Greenwich Egg Company.

'The passenger seat was a pub chair from my local, screwed to the floor! I remember being stopped by police in South London when the tow bar was scraping the tarmac spitting sparks with bricks piled high showing in the rear windows.'

'So when the police drove alongside and read 'Greenwich Egg Company' on the side, they must have thought what came first - the brick or the egg!'

'I took the van with a group of the lads to Yarmouth for the party holiday of a lifetime; the details of that trip remain a legend among the participants, another story!'

Profile:
Tommy is the backbone of BBC's successful Groundforce programme which transforms people's gardens.

He runs his own small building business in Hackney, east London. It specialises in hard landscaping - the part of garden creation that doesn't involve planting.

My first car

'The passenger seat was a pub chair from my local, screwed to the floor! I remember being stopped by police in South London when the tow bar was scraping the tarmac spitting sparks with bricks piled high showing in the rear windows'.

Roger Lloyd-Pack

First car: Morris Minor

It sounds like a motor this rather idiotic Only Fools and Horses character Trigger would try and faithfully keep for life.

'My first car was a beige Morris Minor - HMU565 - given to me by my mother when she got rid of it,' says Roger.

'I hand-painted it a bright green and took it on a tour of Europe. It only just made it back, having to be pushed up the ramp to get on the ferry at Calais. It then just got me home before being sent with full honours on its way!'

My first car

'I hand-painted it a bright green and took it on a tour of Europe. It only just made it back, having to be pushed up the ramp to get on the ferry at Calais. It then just got me home before being sent with full honours on its way!'

Pam Ayres

First car: Morris Minor 1000

Pam Ayres' recollection of her first car - a blue/grey Morris 1000 she bought from her brother for £50 - deserves to be told in her own fabulously poetic words:

Much too slow, and in the way.
You know how much I love you;
I'd repair you in a flash,
But I haven't got the knowledge,
And I haven't got the cash.

There is rust all round your headlamps,
I could push through it if I tried.
My pot of paint can't cure it,
'Cause it's from the other side.
All along the sides and middle,
You are turning rusty brown.

Though you took me ninety thousand miles,
And never let me down.
Not the snapping of a fan belt,
Nor the blowing of a tyre,
Not the rattling of a tappet,
And nor did you misfire.
All your wheels stayed on the corners,
And your wipers on the screen,
Though I didn't do much for you,
And I never kept you clean.

My first car

All of your seats are unupholstered,
And foam rubber specks the floor.
You were hit by something else once,
And I cannot shut the door.
But it's not those things that grieve me,
Or the money that I spent,
For you were my First-driven.

Ninety thousand miles we went.
I could buy a bright and new car,
And go tearing round the town,
A BGT! A Morgan!
(With the hood all battened down).
But as I leave you in the scrapyard,
Bangers piled up to the skies,
Why do your rusty headlamps,
Look like sad, reproachful eyes?

Profile:
Writer, poet, entertainer and broadcaster Pam Ayres has been
delighting the nation with her mix of comic poetry, prose and droll
observations on life for more than twenty years.

She has recently been 'rediscovered', via her appearances on Radio
4's Just a Minute and That Reminds Me.

'But as I leave you in the
scrapyard, Bangers piled up
to the skies, Why do your
rusty headlamps, Look like
sad, reproachful eyes?'

Paul Daniels

First car: Hillman

Paul Daniels started off his car life in his father's Hillman and despite his dad's expert training endured an 'amusing' driving test.

'The car that he owned was the one in which I took my test,' explains Paul. 'To be honest I cannot remember the make of the car although I think it might have been a Hillman. Nowadays the design would be rather strange and I thought it a little odd even then. The boot of the car did not have a door or a lid on the outside.'

'To get into it you had to struggle with your suitcases through the rear of the car, lowering the back of the seat. This was quite a clamber. Also, because of the constant raising and lowering of the back seat, the two catches that held it in place became very worn and were just about useless. Cars were very different then in that they demanded constant attention. They were always breaking down so dad carried a full complement of tools in the boot.'

And it was to be the box of tools in the back that made a sudden, surprise appearance on the day of Paul's test in the car during the emergency stop.

'Dad had said that the examiner would have to look around before shouting 'STOP to make sure that there was nothing behind us, and he did that a few times,' remembers Paul.

'The third time he looked around I quickly checked the mirrors and saw nothing. At the same time the examiner slammed the dashboard and shouted 'STOP' and I did exactly that.

My first car

'The word was not fully out of his mouth before the car was slamming to a standstill. But there was one thing my father and I had forgotten. The two catches on the rear seat gave away under the forward pressure and the back of the back seat crashed down as all the tools and tool boxes in the boot shot forward into the rear of the car with a mighty clatter of metal against metal.'

'The examiner went white, sure that he had missed seeing another vehicle behind us, and sure that he had caused an accident. I am sure that he had had one!

'I passed my test first time. Perhaps he just didn't want to see me, or dad's car, ever again!'

Profile:
Paul Daniels is without doubt one of the most accomplished magicians in the world. Amongst his numerous achievements, he has starred in his own hugely successful West End Theatre Show and headlined in Las Vegas and Broadway.

The Paul Daniels Magic Show was a smash hit on TV and he has also presented Odd One Out, Every Second Counts and Wipe Out.

'I passed my test first time. Perhaps he just didn't want to see me, or dad's car, ever again!'

Lord Montagu

First car: 1947 Hillman Minx

For Lord Montagu of Beaulieu motoring is practically in his blood. His MP father championed the cause of the driver in the first decades of the 20th century and he continued the legacy by setting up one of the finest motor museums in the world.

His own first car experience began at Oxford University when he became the proud owner of a Hillman Minx on his 21st birthday and he used it to travel all over the continent - to France, Italy, Switzerland, Austria and Germany and a three week visit to the Salzburg Festival.

**The following is an excerpt from his book
Wheels Within Wheels:**
'The car was equipped with a green light to indicate that I was in statu pupillari and therefore subject to university regulations. I was only able to buy the car thanks to the cooperation of my friend Brian Rootes, son of the manufacturer's founding father, and pretending that I was still serving abroad in Palestine. This subterfuge meant that the car was officially an 'export model.'

'Nowadays even sixth-formers seem to drive their own cars but in my day there were very few student owner-drivers. I garaged my car in Holywell, in the original Morris Garage from which MG took its name.'

'By happy coincidence many years later when I was chairman of English Heritage...I saw to it that the building was formally listed as being of historical and architectural merit.'

Profile
The present Lord Montagu of Beaulieu is a well known motoring personality who founded Britain's National motor Museum in Beaulieu, Hants, internationally recognised as one of the finest in the world.

The museum holds over 300 exhibits and include world class examples of automotive interest, from early examples of motoring from the 1890's to legendary motor vehicles from all over the world, including record breakers such as 'Bluebird' and 'Golden Arrow'.

My first car

'I was only able to buy the car thanks to the cooperation of my friend Brian Rootes, son of the manufacturer's founding father, and pretending that I was still serving abroad in Palestine.'

Ken Farrington

First car: Austin 7 Ruby

Actor Ken Farrington bought his Austin 7, 1937 Ruby Saloon for just £25 from the father of his school colleague Simon Ward.

The pair were founder members of what is now the National Youth Theatre and it was through that association and Simon's father Len's support for it that led to the car sale.

'It was a real bargain even in those days,' says Ken. 'At the time I was in the Shakespeare history series An Age of Kings and when that finished i went into Coronation Street.

'At that time I took the engine to pieces, renewed the pistons and renovated the whole engine. When finished it was capable of overtaking many a more modern car as it sped up the M1.'

After six months in Coronation Street Ken graduated to a Wolseley. He handed the Ruby on to his brother with disastrous consequences.

'He left it to rot at the end of his builder's yard! For all I know it could still be there in Peckham.'

Profile:
Ken found fame as Annie and Jack Walker's son Billy in Coronation Street. He stayed in the series for 23 years completing 408 episodes.

He has appeared at the National Theatre and with the Royal Shakespeare Company as well as doing tours of India and England.

His credits for other TV programmes are endless but recently he has appeared in Channel 5 soap Family Affairs and ITV1s Emmerdale where he plays Tom King'.

My first car

Tom King
Emmerdale
itv

'At that time I took the engine to pieces, renewed the pistons and renovated the whole engine. When finished it was capable of overtaking many a more modern car as it sped up the M1.'

Linda Bellingham

First car: Ford Anglia

Like many a first car experience, Lynda Bellingham's came to a rather sad end in an accident.

'The car didn't have a name but I really loved it,' says Lynda. 'I used to drive every day to the ATV studios in Elstree. This was 1971 and I was doing a series called General Hospital. I did this for 9 months then one day someone went into the back of my car and pushed me into the car in front, causing the wiring to catch alight and my lovely car was burnt beyond repair. I was so upset.

'I now drive a Mercedes Estate because I have to carry sons, dogs and bikes!'

Profile:
Canadian born actress is a familiar face to TV viewers. Her many credits include General Hospital, All Creatures Great and Small, Doctor Who and Martin Chuzzlewit.

She was also the star of a series of adverts for Oxo cubes playing the 'Oxo mum.'

"The car didn't have a name but I really loved it"

Nick Owen

First car: Ford Anglia

Nick Owen would rather forget his first car experience.

When he first bought it he had to endure an embarrassing drive away from the garage to his flat. 'I was so proud of it at first but as I drove it to my flat it went over a bump and the horn came on and wouldn't go off!' recounts Nick. 'It was so embarrassing driving down the road! In the end I switched off the engine and my friend and I pushed it the last 200 yards.'

So no sooner had he bought the 'dodgy maroon' Ford Anglia for £75 than he was taking it back to the same garage to be told it was unfit for the road.'

He managed to get £70 back for it.

Profile:
Nick Owen is now the main presenter on BBC Midlands Today.

In 1983, he joined TV-am for its launch as sports presenter, but took over the main anchor role within eight weeks.

Here he renewed his partnership with Anne Diamond, and they presented the programme together until late 1986.

Nick then joined ITV Sport as presenter of their flagship programme Midweek Sport Special. He also hosted their Olympic and World Cup coverage, as well as a variety of other sports programmes, including athletics and boxing.

He moved to the BBC in 1992 to present Good Morning With Anne and Nick. When the show finished in 1996 after 600 programmes, Nick presented a variety of programmes around the country.

'It was so embarrassing driving down the road! In the end I switched off the engine and my friend and I pushed it the last 200 yards.'

Bernard Matthews

First car: Austin 7 Van

As the man himself would say - it was simply bootifull!

And from the small beginnings of a business run from an Austin 7 light van emerged an international success story.

Bernard Matthews purchased his Austin 7 light van for the princely sum of £27 and 10 shillings more than 45 years ago.

He used it to pick up feed for his growing flock of turkeys.

And the van was also essential for delivering turkeys and their eggs around the Norwich area.

Profile:
Bernard Matthews Foods Ltd. began in 1950 with 12 turkey eggs and an incubator in the heart of Norfolk.

Although the company's headquarters are still based there, it's business activities stretch into Europe, North America and New Zealand.

The company now produces 13 million turkeys worldwide.

My first car

As the man himself would say - 'it was simply bootifull!'

Bernard Manning

First car: Flying Standard 1933

Its never clever to be cheeky to a policeman even if you can't help it like comedian Bernard Manning.

His first car was a 1933 Flying Standard with a little union jack on the front, old fashioned cord brakes and it was 'two toned black and rust!'

Bernard says: 'I had many good trips in that car to Blackpool, Morecambe etc. A copper pulled me up one time and said 'Is this your car?'. I said, 'It's automatic but I have to be here!' He said 'Does the speedometer work?' and I said 'Only when the wheels are touching the ground!' - that got me two endorsements.'

Bernard got the car by winning a Spot the Ball competition in 1947 and using £30 of the profits.

'It was the best money I ever spent and they were very happy days.'

Profile:
Master joke-teller Bernard found fame in TVs The Comedians and has attracted a firm, devoted following ever since. His colourful language has caused him to be confined to pub and club appearances in recent years but he is still as popular as ever.

My first car

'It was the best money I ever spent and they were very happy days.'

Anthea Turner

First car: Mini

TV presenter Anthea Turner grew very attached to her British Leyland cream Mini and named it 'Champagne Charlie'.

'As with most people who were teenagers in the late 70s, early 80s my first car was a Mini,' says Anthea.

'Its registration was NVT 749W and after my horse, was truly the love of my life. It was polished, cared for and its every whim was pandered to. Our most traumatic time together was when I returned to Charlie after a night out with friends to see him sitting on bricks and his four little wheels stolen! My father came to the rescue as fathers do and ever since I have been obsessed with locking wheel nuts!'

Anthea Turner found fame presenting Top of the Pops and Blue Peter before going on to be a news anchor on GMTV and the BBC's National Lottery Live show.

Now she is setting out to try and re-educate the nation's homemakers in the lost art of keeping the perfect pad on BBC3 'Perfect Housewife'.

My first car

Anthea Turner

'Its registration was NVT 749W and after my horse, was truly the love of my life.'

Mathew Bose

First car: Ford Wrangler Pick-up-truck

Emmerdale actor Mathew Bose took his driving test while living in Los Angeles.

'The test was easier than it is here I have to say, especially as it was in an automatic,' he says. 'Most Americans drive automatics but my first car was in fact an 80s pick-up truck, it was pale blue and it was manual! Much kangarooing around deserted car parks followed till I got the hang of it!'

Mathew developed a great affection for the pick-up, 'Its state of the art entertainment was provided by two mono/tinny speakers fed by a push button cassette player and what was politely known as manual air conditioning actually meant I could never stop moving,' He says.

'But I loved it so much and one of my best life memories is cruising down the freeway to Santa Monica to my acting classes with the warm summer air rushing through the cab and singing along to some trashy pop song at the top of my voice One drawback of a pick-up truck is everyone suddenly becomes your best friend when they need some shopping or help moving house!'

My first car

'Most Americans drive automatics but my first car was in fact an 80s pick-up truck, it was pale blue and it was manual! Much kangarooing around deserted car parks followed till I got the hang of it!'

90

Dominic Littlewood

First car: Ford Cortina MK2

TV presenter Dominic Littlewood had a passion for cars from a young age and passed his driving test aged 17 after just four paid lessons.

His secret for driving success was due to his father who was a former driving instructor and allowed him to drive 40 miles to and from work with L plates in his Citroen 2CV.

'I was working as a city and guilds motor technician apprentice and had purchased a Ford Cortina MK2 a few months prior to my test date,' says Dominic.

'Being a young and enthusiastic mechanic I was practising making alterations and adjustments to the car which didn't need to be done. I jacked the rear end of the car up by 9 inches and put a red light bulb above the rear axle.'

'The rear differential was painted silver and the door panels had red pin stripes put around the edges. I know this sounds ridiculous but it was the fashion in those days, a bit like the present day practice of spoilers and neon lights on the bonnet.'

'In the end I had managed to make such a pig's ear of the car that I never ever got to drive it on the road and ended up selling it for scrap.'

More than 20 years on and Dominic now has a passion for unusual American cars and purchased a Plymouth Prowler 3.5 Lt 24v in a copper tone colour. It is one of only 600 ever made and he exported it back from Pennsylvania, USA to Britain. He also has a Chevrolet SSR, 6.0 Lt.

'I plan on keeping both cars as I have a love of both of them and did not buy them for any money making ideas, purely passion.'

My first car

Profile:
Dominic Littlewood presents To Buy or Not to Buy for BBC One, where buyers are given the chance to 'test-drive' their new home before purchasing.

He's been playing the property market for several years, plus his 15 years' experience as a hard-nosed car dealer has proved very useful when it comes to buying and selling houses.

Dominic made his first TV appearance on Channel 4's Faking It, where he taught a vicar how to be a second-hand car dealer in just one month. He was then drafted in to present BBC Two's Wrong Car Right Car. He's also fronted How I Made My Property Fortune for BBC Two.

He learned about the motor market while working at new and used car dealerships in Essex from the late 1980s, then went on to set up his own company. However, due to increasing media commitments he closed his business down in 2002.

An action man with a hectic schedule, Dominic contributes to car magazines and has written motoring pieces for the press.

'The rear differential was painted silver and the door panels had red pin stripes put around the edges.'

Chris Tarrant

First car: Mini Van

Chris Tarrant's first car was a home too! For four 'very happy' months he lived in his Mini Van after falling out with a girlfriend.

Taken out of his first book, Ken's Furry Friends:
'I'm not quite sure how it actually happened, I remember having a fairly spectacular bust-up with my then girlfriend and roaring off into the night, only to find after about 40 miles I hadn't anywhere to go,' he recounts.

It was winter, it was south-east London and young Chris was teaching English to a motley collection of 'very large West Indians, East Indians, Cypriots, Turks, Greeks, Italians, Irish and about four traditional English skinheads' at the time.

'As you can imagine their domestic backgrounds were varied to say the least, so the fact that 'sir' lived in a Mini Van outside the school didn't bother them much,' says Chris. 'After an initial confrontation when two of them jacked me up on bricks while I lay happily dozing away inside, it all worked very well.'

'I was awakened one night by one of my little lads clanking about under the bonnet: 'Just borrowing your battery, sir, to start my mate's Cooper 'S', promise it'll be back before assembly'. And sure enough it was.'

The van was a bit cramped for the necessary marking a teacher has to do but it was generally cosy. 'I had a mattress, pillow, blankets, and my own little curly-headed alarm clock called Johnston, who used to knock on the windscreen at 7.30 every morning,' says Chris. 'I then used to dive into the school for a nice hot shower and by the time all the other staff crawled in from all over southern England grumbling about traffic jams and British Rail, I was fresh as a daisy.'

Chris' ultimate achievement with the van was getting the post delivered!

After several weeks of hassle with GPO Head Office, the first delivery was magic,' he says. 'There was this scratching on the thick ice on the windscreen and a voice enquiring 'Mr Tarrant?' and as I slid open the little Mini window there it was on the envelope: C.J. Tarrant Esq, 161 GLO, Sprules Road, London SE4.' But there was a drawback to the van - it was far from a smash hit with the ladies - and living in it had to come to an end.'

'Conversations like 'Shall we go back to your place?, 'Well...actually, we're in it!' I could handle, and most of the ladies came to terms with the idea that 'Popping upstairs' meant climbing.'

Profile:
After a period of extreme poverty, including living in the van for a period, Chris Tarrant wrote to local TV stations until someone took notice.

He came to national prominence through kids gunge show Tiswas and its adult spin-off, OTT. He was a fiercely loyal stalwart of Capital FM, where he was a disc jockey since the 1980s.

Since then, he has hosted numerous TV shows, including the hugely popular Who Wants to be a Millionaire on ITV1.

My first car

'I had a mattress, pillow, blankets, and my own little curly-headed alarm clock called Johnston, who used to knock on the windscreen at 7.30 every morning'.

Raji James

First car: Austin Allegro

Eastenders actor Raji James had an all too familiar start to driving life as for many of Britain's young Asians.

He remembers the first time he went out with his mates in his Austin Allegro which had been his mum's.

'I managed to get stopped by the police on four different occasions in the same evening!' he says. 'The final time happened while I was parked outside my friends' house saying goodbye to them. The police thought I was a burglar!'

Profile:
Raji James plays Ash Ferreira in BBC soap Eastenders. He was also in The Bill and his biggest role is starring in the big screen flick East Is East.

'I managed to get stopped by the police on four different occasions in the same evening!'

Paul Barber

First car: Singer Sunbeam Convertible

Yes it does sound like a scene straight from Only Fools and Horses.

It is 1970 and a group of mates set off for Newcastle in a car given to one of them as a gift.

New owner Paul Barber, who played Denzil in the hit BBC comedy, explains the rest.

'It was 11 O'clock at night and 'pissing' down with rain - the roof kept blowing open! 'We all had fur coats on as we were hippies. Yet by the end of the night we all looked like a bunch of stray animals.

'It died on reaching Newcastle five hours later and I am now very wary of convertibles!'

My first car

'It was 11 o-clock at night
and pissing down with
rain - the roof kept
blowing open! 'We all
had fur coats on as we
were hippies!'

Ian Carmichael

First car: Ford Consul

For Ian Carmichael, the wait for his own first car was a long one.

He took his driving test in 1928 in a Vauxhall in his home town of Hull and passed. He was 17 or 18, still at boarding school and was 'delighted' to have passed. But he did not have his own car.

'I lived at home and in the holidays I drove my mother's Morris,' says Ian. 'Returning home from the test I drove my father in his Ford V8 - quite a powerful machine after the Vauxhall - and I was feeling cock-a-hoop. I felt as if I had achieved manhood.'

He did not own a car of his own until he was in his early 30's by which time he was married with two small daughters.

'My wife collected it from the dealer and drove out to Pinewood Studios with my daughters to pick me up at the end of the day's shooting,' remembers Ian.

'It was a brand new Ford Consul, 474 FHX. I was very fond of it and it certainly improved the Carmichael family transport situation. To me it was a Rolls Royce!'

Profile:
A light comedian from stage revue, Ian Carmichael took the British cinema by storm in the 1950s, and established himself as a major star. Kingsley Amis's Lucky Jim, I'm All Right Jack and School for Scoundrels.

He appeared in two television sagas, one playing P.G. Wodehouse's Bertie Wooster.

Photo: Richard Welford-Smith. Scarborough

For Chris ——
Every good wish Ian Carmichael

'It was a brand new Ford Consul, 474 FHX. I was very fond of it and it certainly improved the Carmichael family transport situation. To me it was a Rolls Royce!'

Mollie Sugden

First car: Singer

Mollie Sugden received her first car for the saddest of reasons - her father's death.

Her elder brother already had a Jaguar so he suggested that Mollie take her dad's six-month-old Singer.

'I kept it for a couple of years then did a straight trade for a Morris Minor, a new sweet little car,' says Mollie.

'Since then I have always been lucky enough to have new cars. I cannot remember them all but they include a Ford Anglia, a Ford Cortina Estate (to carry all the twin babies' equipment), a Hillman Estate and a Ford Capri.

'In the last 20 years I have had a BMW, a Porsche and two Mercedes. As you may guess I love motor cars!'

My first car

Profile:
Mollie is a stalwart of British comedy drama, and her credits include: Hugh and I, Please Sir!, Doctor in The House, For The Love Of Ada, Mrs Hutchinson in The Liver Birds, Mrs Slocombe (complete with pussy) in Are You Being Served? and Grace and Favour, Whodunnit?, Come Back Mrs Noah, Tea Ladies, That's My Boy, Cludeo and Oliver's Travels and Little Britain.

Photo: BBC

'I kept it for a couple of years then did a straight trade for a Morris Minor, a new sweet little car'.

Michael Grade

First car: Riley 1.5

All too often first cars come a cropper but luckily for Michael Grade he emerged unscathed from his prang.

He was driving his Riley - which his dad had bought for his 18th birthday in 1961 - back from a football match when he skidded on black ice.

'It turned over and ended up in a ditch,' he remembers. 'I didn't hit anything and luckily the passenger and I were unhurt. Good cars, those Rileys!'

Profile:
Michael Grade was appointed BBC chairman in 2004. He is a former controller of BBC One and Channel 4.

He comes from a showbusiness family, having television mogul Lord Grade, a pioneer of ITV, as his uncle.

As well as being director of programmes at London Weekend Television and BBC Television, he went on to head the merged Pinewood and Shepperton film studios.

As BBC One controller in the 1980s, he launched top-rating soap Eastenders - but axed sci-fi favourite Doctor Who.

Photo: BBC

'I didn't hit anything and luckily the passenger and I were unhurt. Good cars, those Rileys!'

Neil Buchanan

First car: Fiat Uno

Neil Buchanan describes his Fiat Uno as 'rather boring' and not worth the 3-month wait to pick it up from a dealership in Purley, Surrey.

So let's go back to his first driving experience - in his girlfriend's car, the make of which he cannot remember. It had been bought for her by her wealthy parents and he was not supposed to drive it. 'My girlfriend and I adhered to their wishes - well, at least she did,' admits Neil. 'I used to 'borrow' it occasionally without her knowing!'

'I admit now it was not the most honourable thing to do and I almost came unstuck once when, as an inexperienced driver, I smashed a wing mirror.'

'I then had about 4 hours to get it to the garage and begged them to change it there and then, which they duly obliged.'

'I made it back with half an hour to spare, so she was never the wiser. It is not something I would ever do again and I did learn my lesson!'

Profile:
Neil Buchanan has appeared in and presented a number of children's TV shows and is most famous for Art Attack on CITV.

My first car

'I admit now it was not the most honourable thing to do and I almost came unstuck once when, as an inexperienced driver, I smashed a wing mirror'.

Jerome Flynn

First car: Volvo 122 Estate

There is nothing quite like a mother's love and the weakness they have for their pleas.

'My first car was a volvo, it belonged to my mother. I used to borrow it all the time.'

'In the end after much persistence I went on to adopt it and loved it very much' says Jerome.

'I passed my test first time. How? I don't know as I drove right up onto the kerb while reversing.'

Profile:
Jerome Flynn has appeared in a number of films and TV programmes but his biggest success was Soldier Soldier, in which he starred alongside Robson Green.

A performance of Unchained Melody in an episode of the drama launched him and co-star Green onto a short, but successful, pop career.

My first car

'I passed my test first time despite reversing up onto the kerb!'

Pat Moss

First car: Morris Minor

You have heard of driving star Stirling Moss but his sister Pat was a fast mover too - she became the world's leading female rallyist.

Her first car was a Morris Minor 10 or 12 and coloured black and green. 'The doors opened the opposite way to a modern day car and the registration number was NG3 533,' she says.

'The car was looked after and tuned by my brother Stirling's mechanic. From then on I entered rallies until my car died on me.'

'Then I got a triumph TR2, it was white with a red interior and it became the end of what I called my 'private cars'.'

'From then on I had what we call 'factory cars'. The companies I used to rally for loaned them out to me for my own use and I have never had a private car of my own since.'

Profile:
Pat Moss-Carlsson is one of the most famous women in motorsport. Sister of Stirling Moss, her rally driving career in the 1950s and 1960s brought her victories in prestigious events such as the Liège-Rome-Liège, the German and Tulip rallies, not to mention countless Coupes des Dames.

Stirling's sister Pat, inherited her mother's love of horses and duly became a noted show jumping champion.

My first car

'The doors opened the opposite way to a modern day car and the registration number was NG3 533'.

Christopher Casenove

First car: Wolseley 1949

You cannot avoid the inevitable - your first car always conks out completely at some point.

Christopher Cazenove bought his 20-year-old Wolseley for £10 as a student and it served him well, for a while!

'It was the 4-cylinder version of the one used by the police and it looked identical to the police cars you see in the movies of the period,' says Christopher. Its top speed was not much in excess of 40mph however and a couple of long journeys too many caused its demise.'

'I was taking a fellow drama student from Bristol to London for an interview. I was pushing the old girl a bit and there was a sudden, rather nasty noise from the engine,' recalls Christopher.

'We just about made our way slowly into London. But a couple of days later I was off to Plymouth where we were to perform 3 plays and I decided to drive, although I knew she was on her last legs.'

'My intention was to get her to Plymouth, find a cliff and let her plunge into the sea below (I was still an irresponsible student!).'

'I drove it very slowly with the engine making a terrible clanking sound. Then just after midnight near Ilminster there was a huge explosion and the car ground to a halt.'

'With the help of my torch I discovered there were large holes either side of the crank case and chunks of metal littered the road behind me!'

'I dossed down in the car for the night and the next morning, with the help of a local farmer organised for her to be towed to the nearest scrapyard, and did the rest of my journey on the train.'

Profile:
He trained at drama school in Bristol, before moving to Battersea, London in 1969.

Christopher decided to become an actor after he was rejected as officer material by the Navy.

A TV and film regular on both sides of the Atlantic since the 1970s, Christopher's most recently been seen in Judge John Deed. His other notable credits include The Duchess of Duke Street, Dynasty, and the films Heat and Dust and Three Men and a Little Lady.

For many years, Christopher was cast as turn-of-the century aristocrats with military leanings, reflecting his upper middle class background. His early roles included Lt Richard Gaunt in The Regiment and George Cornwallis-West in Jennie: Lady Randolph Churchill.

He found fame as Charlie in the 1970s mini-series The Duchess of Duke Street.

My first car

'My intention was to get her to Plymouth, find a cliff and let her plunge into the sea below (I was still an irresponsible student!).'

Tony Hancock

First car: Mercedes Coupe 1934

Legendary comedian Tony Hancock named his car after his own favourite funny man.

His Mercedes Coupe was named 'Sid' after the comedian Sid Field.

His brother Roger says: 'He had two more Mercedes after that. The sad thing is though he never learned to drive!'

My first car

Profile:
Tony Hancock's career took off on the radio. Hancock's Half Hour kicked off in November 1954 becoming a very British, comic-institution for almost two decades.

By 1956, the series had become so successful it transferred to TV and the comic sitcom as we know it was born.

Hancock is regarded by many as the greatest radio and television comedian of his day. He died in 1968.

'He had two more Mercedes after that. The sad thing is though he never learned to drive!'

Ainsley Harriott

First car: Singer Imp

Ainsley Harriott loves his cars as much as his cooking.

'My first car was a Super Imp that used to belong to my mum and it was known in the family as Betsy,' says Ainsley.

'That was followed by a Ford Mk III, a Fiat, a BMW 18 left hand drive and the list goes on and on.'

'It was a great first car. It gave me independence, the radio was really loud and I had my own private space - it was truly ace.'

Profile:
Ainsley Harriott is the charismatic, larger than life presenter of BBC Two's Ready Steady Cook.

He has worked in top restaurants, as a caterer to celebrities, a singer and a comedian on radio and TV.

My first car

Ainsley Harriott

'My first car was a Super Imp that used to belong to my mum and it was known in the family as Betsy'.

Richard Thorp

First car: MG-TC

Thoughts about my first car take me back to when I owned a (MG TC) that I brought from my brother. At that particular time I was living with my parents in Surrey. We owned a family shoe business, but my heart wasn't really in it and I had other ambitions of being an Actor. I still have fond memories of driving back and forth to Drama School in the MG-TC.

'My first break into show business came when I was offered a main role in the film 'The Dam Busters' - Squadron Leader Mudsley. I then followed a career into Radio and then into Television where I landed a part in 'Emergency Ward IO'.

'By this time I'd had a number of different cars—in fact when I arrived at work each day other members of the cast would peep through the windows to see which one I was driving—My love of cars fascinated them'.

'During the 60's and 70's period I had a great fun with my E. Type Jaguar, but my favourite was a Ferrari Dino which I drove to and from Surrey-Manchester to take part in a TV Series called 'A Family at War'.

'On one memorable occasion I visited my father who at the time lived in Torquay; I drove the three hours at 130mph...It was great fun!!'

Profile:
At the present time Richard owns a Cadillac and a Peugeot 206. He currently travels from South Wales (where he now lives) to Yorkshire TV for his part in Emmerdale.

He say's, 'I am not the highest paid soap star but I do get a good salary based on my film status. I only appear now and again to say a few lines. But the pay allows me to continue to live out one of my life's passions—maintaining and running cars.'

My first car

Photo: BBC

Alan Turner

'On one memorable occasions I visited my father who at the time lived in Torquay; I drove the three hours at 130mph...It was great fun!!'

The Beverly Sisters

First car: Rolls Royce

They were the original Spice girls! The Beverley Sisters were in fact the first British girl group to break into the American Top Ten charts in 1956!

The Sisters are a household name and during their long career they gained the honour of being the most successful sister act ever on television. They are real sisters. Teddie and Babs being identical twins born on their sister's Joy's birthday.

'Until Joy married the famous Billy Wright, England football captain our dad always drove us or we had a chauffeured car to do all our many long journeys. One year while on a record breaking season at Gt Yarmouth we brought our very own first Rolls Royce.'

'During a publicity photo shoot we discovered that the drivers of the horse drawn carriages (that took holiday makers along the front) had a vast quantity of lovely manure which we craved for our new London garden.'

My first car

'One particular weekend when Bill's car was being serviced he came up in our car to visit Joy. While he was there we took the opportunity to fill the huge boot of our Rolls Royce with as many dirty great sacks of this precious stuff as it would hold.'

A week later Billy drove up again and we once more decided to get another load, but just imagine our 'shock horror' when we found that the boot was still full with last weeks piles!'

'During that week Billy has been honoured with an invitation to lunch with the Queen at Buckingham Palace and had parked the Rolls with all the smelly manure still in it under the Queen's window.'

'We laughed so much and knew then why he hadn't been knighted!'

Profile:
After being discovered in 1944 by the biggest musical name of the time Glenn Miller they shot to stardom. The Beverley Sisters had a wonderful life in show business playing and topping the bill of many famous venues around the world. As well has having their own TV Series for seven years they broke box-office records for more than a decade as Britain's highest paid female act. Their recording hits included 'Sisters', 'I saw Mummy kissing Santa Claus', 'Drummer Boy', 'Little Donkey' and many more.

'We laughed so much and knew then why he hadn't been knighted!'

Norman Wisdom OBE

First car: Black Morgan

Norman Wisdom managed to make millions of people laugh most of his life and so it didn't seem to out of the ordinary when he laughed throughout the tale of his first car.

Norman didn't start out in a car; in fact his first mode of transport was a BSA 350CC motor bike which he brought when he arrived back in England after coming out of the army in India.

'It was just after getting my first stage job in the Collins Music hall Islington that I proudly brought my first car which was a super little black Morgan', he recalls. 'It was second hand of course but was a stunner and didn't half pull the birds. No I'm not telling you what we got up to in it as this is a family book!'

'It took me everywhere, even to the film studios where I made my first film 'Trouble in Store' with the lovely late great Margaret Rutherford. Do you know we laughed so much making that film and had tremendous fun, just as my little car gave me!'

'One day the drivers seat collapsed while driving and me being on the short side sank into it and it looked like, as my eyes disappeared under the dashboard a little kid driving. It also made a strange noise when we went round corners. It was as though something was rolling in the back, it only stopped making the noise when it was full of petrol. When I took it to the garage they discovered a marble in the tank!'

Profile:

Slapstick comedian Norman Wisdom born in 1917 is a former Army flyweight boxing champion. Since making his leap into showbiz after leaving the army in 1946 at the age of 31 he rose with spectacular speed and he was a West End star within two years.

His success made him a natural for TV and then came the films that made him such an icon. Wisdom created one of the most continuing characters in screen comedy; the unsystematic, loser in an ill-fitting suit and tuned-up cap that struggled to get anything right in life.

He was a comedy legend of black 'n' white TV and pictures and took semi retirement in 1980 when he moved to the Isle of Man. His retirement wasn't his final stage in his great career and recent recognised parts in the likes of Coronation Street, Last Of The Summer Wine and the big-screen versions of Five Children and It revived his profile.

Yet Knighthood in 2000 as he will always be known as the awkward, well-meaning man with the signature tune 'Don't Laugh At Me 'Cos I'm A Fool'.

My first car

'It was second hand of course but was a stunner and didn't half pull the birds. No I'm not telling you what we got up to in it as this is a family book!'

John Evans

First car: Mßini cc

John Evans is renowned for balancing anything that can be imagined on his head! This is exactly what he done with his first car.

'My first car was a Mini which was very low cost to run but seemed a fast ride being so close to the ground.'

'I was once going to the seaside and got a flat tyre, after realising I had no jack in the car I decided to lifted the mini up instead to put on the spare.'

Profile:
John Evans made his début of head balancing in 1993 when he balanced a mini car on his head on a television show titled 'Fantastic facts' hosted by Jonathan Ross. Since then he has travelled the world balancing minis' and other objects on his head.

Just some of the objects include: 548 footballs, 11 beer kegs, 95 milk crates and 225 pints of beer.

John is currently the undefeated head-balancing champion.

My first car

'My first car was a Mini which was very low cost to run but seemed a fast ride being so close to the ground'.

Rula Lenska

First car: Austin Healey

Oh it's so much more fun when parents don't know what we are up to and that's exactly the case of Roza-Marie Leopoldnya Lubienska as she was known then.

'My first car was an Austin Healy ex-police car and I brought it before I could even drive', she recalls, 'unbeknown to my parents I used to drive it around The Kilburn area'.

'I brought it for £100 which was a lot of money in 1971; it had bullet holes in the dashboard, or so I was told! I used to play at being a car mechanic trying to mend a very noisy exhaust. I kept the car until by chance a mechanic acquaintance informed me that the chassis was cracked and that it could have literally disintegrated at any moment! I had brought this car from a so called friend!'

'One of the numerous funny occasions was, late one night driving down the Kilburn High Road with a girlfriend we were pulled over for having a missing headlight. The policeman (young and very handsome) walked around the car and asked for my documents – I didn't have any! He asked why there wasn't a tax disc – I didn't have one! Insurance – Again none! Finally the policeman said 'we could throw the book at you for this', but he didn't and just cautioned me instead'.

The funny thing was he and I stayed good friends for many years after this'.

Profile:
Rula Lenska was brought to our TV screens again in 2006 as a member of Celebrity Big Brother's house; however she has been a house hold name since the 70's. Her first acting job was a thriller, which started life in Windsor, and she played a murderess au pair!

Some of her greatest TV hits have been 'Take a letter Mr Jones'; Mr H is late; Kappatoo and the unforgettable 'The Rock Follies' the Thames Television show from the 70's that followed the fortunes of 'The Little Ladies'.

Photo: JEAN-PHILIPPE DEFAUT

'I brought it for £100 which was a lot of money in 1971; it had bullet holes in the dashboard, or so I was told! I used to play at being a car mechanic trying to mend a very noisy exhaust.'

Michelle Hardwick

First car: Ford Escort

Michelle acted no differently than any other young girl on her 18th birthday when her parents presented her with her first car on 24th February 1994.

'I was so excited about my car, they had brought it from my Auntie Janet, gave it a re spray and spruced it up for me'. She said

My first car

'It was a red 'C' registration Ford Escort and I even gave her a name' I couldn't actually drive when I first got her and it took me six attempts to pass my driving test. I did pass eventually within the year though, thank god!'

'I will never forget my first car as she was great to drive and helped build my confidence on the road; her name was 'Saffy!'.

Profile:
Michelle Hardwick is best known for her role as Lizzie Kennoway in the popular ITV drama series The Royal.

She now drives a Citroen XSARA; 'maybe my next car will be a sports car; who knows!'.

'I was so excited about my car, they had brought it from my Auntie Janet, gave it a re spray and spruced it up for me'.

Sir Digby Jones

First car: Fiat 126

The phrase 'Give us a lift!' has the overall edge on Sir Digby's story.

'I passed my driving on 5 December 1972, just over a month after my 17th birthday. I borrowed my sister's mini for three years while saving up for my own car by doing various holiday jobs.'

On 1 August 1975 I finally had enough money to buy a car. I brought a Fiat 126, registration number MUY 161P. At the time it was the cheapest new car that you could buy in Britain, it has a 594cc engine in the back. There have been more powerful lawnmowers made since! However I was thrilled to have it.'

'In the summer of 1976 I took the car on a camping holiday around Europe, getting as far south as Barcelona. I still had the car when I

was a law student at UCL and remember one particular incident when I had parked it on a meter outside the university. Three guys picked it up between them, carried it into the law faculty, put it in a lift and sent it to the top floor'.

'I owned the car until February 1978. The car was well used in the three years and by the time I sold it had driven 65,000 miles.'

Profile:
It was in corporate finance and client development that Digby Jones made his name and he is known today as the 'voice of business'. As the Chief Executive of the UK's 'voice of business', he regularly visits businesses across the world, taking their views back to those who make the rules. He has taken the British business message to over 60 different countries.

He is a President, Member and Chairman of many different associations such as; UNICEF, Cancer research UK, WellChild, Mencap's WorkRight initiative, National Learning and Skills Council.

His business chorizema has helped raise millions of pounds for charities in the UK and adding to his many credits he was appointed a Knight Bachelor in the 2005 New Year Honours List.

My first car

'On 1 August 1975 I finally had enough money to buy a car. I brought a Fiat 126, registration number MUY 161P'.

Sir Patrick Moore CBE

First car: Ford Prefect

Talk about keeping your eye on it! That's exactly what Sir Patrick Moore has done with his first car.

'My First car was a Ford Prefect, registration number GPN 924, known to all as 'The Ark'. I have done over 600,000 miles in it and am proud to say I still have it.'

'I do not have any bizarre stories of the car, just that it has been as faithful to me as I have to it. It has to have a windscreen repair but other than that 'The Ark' is still in full working action!'

Profile:
Between the ages of six to sixteen Patrick was educated from home due to illness. And it was throughout this time he read a copy of 'The Story of the Solar System' which sparked his love for astronomy. Since then, he has concentrated upon studies of the Moon.

He is also the inspiration behind the hugely successful TV program The Sky at Night. Since April 1957, he has presented every one of the monthly Sky at Night programmes. This has earned him a place in the 'Guinness book of Records' as the longest serving television presenter. At the time of the first ever broadcast the sky was graced by the presence of a bright comet, Arend-Roland. All this took place months before the launch of Sputnik 1 and long before the 'space race'.

In 1959, the Russians used his charts to correlate the first Lunik 3 pictures of the far side of the Moon and he was involved in the lunar mapping before the NASA Apollo missions.

Over the years Patrick has written in excess of 60 books on astronomy.

My first car

'I do not have any bizarre stories of the car, just that it has been as faithful tome as I have to it.'

Chris Crew

'In the 1970's I was living in Southampton, I wasn't very happy there so I decided to return to my home town of Nottingham. I needed transport and was short of cash so I swapped a portable colour TV for a grey Bullnose Morris Oxford, 501 NIK. Unfortunately the car wasn't taxed or insured, but that wasn't going to deter me from driving back to Nottingham.'

'I reasoned that if I painted the car all the colours of the rainbow the police wouldn't stop me. After all they re bound to think to themselves 'anyone who paints his car like that doesn't mind attracting attention and must have all the right documents!'

'Setting off for Nottingham felling quite confident, I travelled down the busy roads; other motorists flashed their lights and honked their horns to demonstrate their approval for my highly decorated car. Even pedestrians smiled and waved at me but then suddenly my confidence took a nose dive. About two hundred yards ahead of me stood two policemen beside a parked police van. Their eyes caught mine and one of the policemen gave me a stop sign and motioned me to pull over to the side of the road. I thought to myself, 'you're in trouble now.' My car came to a stuttering halt and as I wound the window down a smiling policeman approach me saying 'don't worry lad, you've done nothing wrong. We're only stopping cars at random to check their tyres and we'd be grateful if you would cooperate?'

'I reluctantly agreed to their tyre checks, after about five minutes of examining the car one of the policemen popped his head through the window and said, 'this is an old car lad, what kind is it ?' My voice croaked out a reply, 'it's a Bullnose Morris Oxford'. Smiling he said, 'you can't really tell under all that paint, are you an artist?' 'Yes.' I said rather nervously. He put his hand on his chin and thought for a moment; 'here we go' I thought 'he's going to ask for my documents'. 'your tyres are perfect sir. I just wondered if you'd allow us to take a photo of you and your car for the

My first car

police gazette as its so unusual?' How could I resist! They told me to stand in front of the number plate so the car can't be traced and took the photo. After they thanked me kindly and waved me on my way. I drove away with a great sense of relief.'

Eventually I reached my destination. Driving down the high road I could see a man on crutches about to cross the road. I braked so he could cross, but the car continued and knocked him over. I could actually feel the car rolling over his body, I thought 'you've blinking killed him'. I jumped out of the car and saw the poor man trapped underneath it. I said rather stupidly, 'are you alright?' but then I noticed his legs had been separated from his body! 'my god, you've cut him in two!' I shouted. And suddenly the man pulled himself from under the car, 'don't worry, I'm alright, these are pot legs.' I nearly fainted with relief, trying not to laugh as I helped to put him back together. I drove the poor man home and we actually became good friends and still often laugh about it.

I still have not passed my test due to my dyslexia. I do sometimes get behind the wheel but get confused with my left and right turns.

This is a copy of the first letter Chris tried to draft to contact celebrities. 'I had to get someone to type this letter for me.'